KU-040-387

The Heart at Rest

'Enfolded in Love' series
General Editor: Robert Llewelyn

THE HEART AT REST

Daily Readings with St Augustine of Hippo

Introduced and edited by
Dame Maura Sée OSB
Illustrated by Irene Ogden

Darton, Longman and Todd
London

First published in 1986 by
Darton, Longman and Todd Ltd
89 Lillie Road, London SW6 1UD

Introduction and arrangement
© 1986 Dame Maura Sée OSB
Illustrations © 1986 The Julian Shrine

ISBN 0 232 51673 1

British Library Cataloguing in Publication Data

Augustine, *Saint, Bishop of Hippo*
The heart at rest: daily readings with
St. Augustine of Hippo.——(Enfolded in
love series)
1. Devotional calendars
I. Title   II. Sée, (*Dame*), Maura
III. Series
242'.2   BV4810

ISBN 0–232–51673–1

Phototypeset by Input Typesetting Ltd,
London SW19 8DR
Printed and bound in Great Britain by
Anchor Brendon Ltd, Tiptree, Essex

'Thou hast made us for thyself, and our hearts
are restless till they rest in thee'

St Augustine

Contents

Introduction

Augustine was born in 354 at Thagaste, a prosperous town in North Africa. His family were what would now be called impoverished gentlefolk, devoted to their children and prepared to make great sacrifices to give them the education which opened the door to a successful career. His father Patricius was a pagan – an affectionate father but a hot tempered husband. His mother Monica has to some extent become the legendary Christian mother. She was a submissive wife, but no weakling as a parent. After schooling in Thagaste and Madaura, Augustine went in 371 to Carthage, the second city of the Western Empire, to complete his education; and it was there that his intellectual and moral tergiversations began. However, the dramatic picture of his conversion from a life of libertinism has little foundation in fact: young men from the provinces suddenly moving into the freedom of a university town are unlikely to conform to the standards of Victorian morality, but there is no reason to suppose that Augustine in his longing for love, and the intensity of his emotional make up – he wept with Dido at Aeneas' departure – was more involved than any young man of his time and world; and he hated the rowdiness and violence of his fellow students.

Romanianus, a friend of his father, was a rich and well-born Roman landowner, and it was to his patronage that the young man owed the first successful steps in his career, as a teacher of rhetoric in Rome. The model of the period was the advocate, the accomplished orator of the Ciceronian type, and Augustine's natural talents and charm fitted him admirably for the role. After a year in Rome, a splendid future opened before him: while still at Carthage he had attracted the notice of Symmachus the Proconsul, and the latter, now Prefect of Rome, offered him the important post of Professor of Rhetoric at Milan, the seat of the Imperial court. He describes this step as I went to 'Milan . . . and to Ambrose'. That great bishop, who incidentally was a cousin of the pagan Symmachus, was the outstanding figure in the Church of the West, the hammer of the Arians, the pedagogue of Emperors, and the classical exponent of Christian doctrine. Augustine looks back on this move from years later, but it sums up his state of mind at the time. His had ever been a search for ultimate reality, but none of the philosophies he had absorbed had satisfied him. In spite of his mother's teaching and example Christianity had passed him by; but now he began to draw a little nearer to it, sitting at Ambrose's feet. He was put off by what, to a civilized Roman, seemed the vulgarity of the Scriptures on a first reading, but he gradually became convinced that the truth he had sought for so long was there within his grasp.

A great difficulty remained: intellectual conviction had led him to the threshold of the Christian faith, but its demands went further. 'The man who loves the world' – its ambitions and its sensual pleasures – 'is an enemy of God.' With Augustine it had to be all or nothing, and it is perhaps in his account of his final conversion in the garden at Milan, that he seems nearest to our modern anguishes with 'shall it never be lawful again?'

Monica had been busy arranging a suitable marriage for the brilliant future; she had got rid of the concubine who had been Augustine's companion for fifteen years, and we should do well not to look at the world of 386 with the eyes of today: a concubine was not a common law wife, but a mistress-cum-housekeeper, an arrangement recognized and taken for granted in the Roman world. Augustine resolved to give himself wholly to God; the marriage plan was given up, and he and a group of friends and pupils retired to a country estate at Cassiciacum to meditate on the eternal truths and prepare for baptism. They were baptized by Ambrose at Easter 386.

He then returned to Rome with Monica, on their way back to North Africa. In a most moving passage of the *Confessions* Augustine describes his mother's last days at Ostia: a mystical experience they shared, her death, and his overwhelming sorrow. He went back to Carthage in 388, and finally with a group of brilliant and like minded friends settled at Thagaste. Augustine had always been attracted by the monastic ideal, and these 'servants of God' as they were called, seemed to embody the life he found most congenial. However, in 391, on a visit to a friend in Hippo Regis, he was, against his inclinations, ordained priest to the old Bishop Valerius. For five years he lived in Hippo in community – 'the monastery in the garden' it was called – but on the death of

Valerius, became himself bishop, and ruled the diocese for thirty-four years.

On the sack of Rome in 410 he was faced with an influx of aristocratic refugees, which presented the kind of problems with which the Second World War made us familiar. But in 429 the end of its world came to North Africa. The Vandals from Spain poured across the straits of Gibraltar and devastated the rich province. They besieged Hippo in 430 as the old bishop lay dying. He had the 'four Psalms of David that deal with penance' fastened to the wall where he could see them from his bed, and for the last ten days he would receive no visitors so that he might weep and pray alone, and on 28 August 430 he went to God.

THE MAN AND HIS TEACHING

Perhaps no one since the writers of the New Testament has had so wide ranging an influence on Christian life and thought in all its aspects as St Augustine. Sixteen centuries separate us from his world, but if we look more closely we shall see that the problems which faced him are those of every age of the Church, and his teaching as relevant to our day as to his. He was the shepherd of a very mixed flock: Christians of various degrees of fervour and conviction, intellectually able pagans, waverers nominally Christian but hedging their bets by clinging to their pagan background and habits. Hippo was a big commercial port, and the bishop and his teaching was as accessible to the dockers as to the notables. Though Christianity had been the official religion of the Empire for over a century, it was not the natural background to the life of his flock in the way that it was the underlying reality of the Middle Ages; he had to inculcate what we should consider the basic principles of Christian morality, and at the same time lead those who sought them to the heights of the love of God. He was in a strong position to do so – there was no danger of copybook teaching from their bishop's chair – he knew from experience the path, with its signposts and pitfalls, from this world's values to those of the kingdom of Heaven, and in a 'trembling flash' had caught a glimpse of the end of the journey.

When he became bishop he was faced with a large-scale schism which threatened to disrupt the African Church. The Donatist (the sect took their name from Donatus, the intruded Bishop of Carthage) was in a sense the paradigm of the Schismatic; he started out from the sound if rigorous principle that a bishop who had yielded under persecution was unworthy of his office and should no longer hold it. A not dissimilar situation arose after the Second World War, when political or moral pressure forced the resignation of certain prelates. But the Donatists went further: such treachery, they held, annihilated the traitor's episcopal powers, his ordinations were of no effect and the sacraments he celebrated non existent. All this might have remained on a theoretical if heretical level – had not the great St Cyprian held that baptism administered by a heretic was null and void and it had needed the Pope's authority to say he was mistaken – but the Donatists went further and held that anyone holding communion with the traitor or those he had ordained was no longer part of the true Church. It was a doctrine that was to crop up again: the distinction between the 'pure', the *élite* and the rest; it might even be possible today to catch a whiff of it in Archbishop Lefevre's conventicles.

Augustine rose to the challenge characteristically: he met the arguments first on rational grounds. Was it likely that the true Church existed only in a small group led by the bishop of a provincial see? The Church of the apostles had spread throughout the world. Was it to be supposed that the Holy Spirit was no longer with it? But it was in declaring the faith of the Church that not only the line he took, but almost his very words, became part of the rule of faith for Christians throughout the centuries. Augustine thundered from his chair that it is Christ who baptizes, ordains, consecrates, not Peter or Augustine or Judas. That was where the Donatists were wrong on the facts, but the sin of the schismatic, he said, goes deeper: the primacy of love was the recurring theme of his gospel, God's love for us ineluctably calls forth our love for him and our fellow men. The members of the Church are united to Christ their head and to one another by the bond of love, and anything that destroys the unity of the Church destroys that bond. So convincing were the bishop's arguments that from a powerful and militant majority the Donatists became an aggressive minority. At this point Augustine enforced the State's repression of heresy with its heavy civil penalties. From our twentieth-century liberal point of view it is a line difficult to defend, but the separation of Church and State is a comparatively modern idea, and even today in Spain and Eire the bishops have looked to the State for moral and legal support.

There is nothing new or startling in what Augustine says. He teaches the Christian faith, but puts it forth with a forcefulness, a brilliancy, and a charm which have seldom been equalled. The fourth and fifth centuries were notable for two trends of deviant Christian belief against which his genius traced out the path of orthodoxy. Some forty years before he was born the teaching of Arius had been condemned at the Council of Nicea. It might seem merely an obscure theological point, but in fact, as Augustine saw with his usual clarity, it undermined the fundamentals of Christian belief: if Jesus Christ was not coequal and coeternal with the Father, then God had not become man for our salvation, and if he were only the most exalted of God's creatures, we could not worship the Trinity of Three Persons in one God. In one form or another this heresy has persisted throughout the history of Christianity, down to *The Myth of God Incarnate* in our own time. Augustine's refutation still remains one of the most potent. He saw that belief in the divinity of Christ demands that faith which enables us to cling to a God whom we cannot yet see, and he tells us that when our Lord said 'blessed are they who have not seen and yet have believed' he was speaking to us. His usual weapon in controversy was God's revelation of himself in the Scriptures; against Arius he reiterates the Evangelist's word 'in the beginning was the Word and the Word was with

God and the Word was God . . . and the Word was made flesh and dwelt among us' and he is never tired of pointing out to his hearers how often our Lord spoke of his relationship to the Father.

The second danger to the Faith that Augustine met was to have broad and deep ramifications throughout later centuries, and its echoes can be heard today in the activist and self-fulfilling Christianity of our times. The Catholic faith holds that man can do no good deed, resist no temptation, take no step on the path to union with God, except with the aid of grace freely offered by God. It is also a fact of common experience that this grace can be accepted or refused. The question is how does this happen? Pelagius, a British monk, put forth the theory that the acceptance or refusal of grace depended on man's volition alone. Augustine met this by his insistence that grace is needed to accept the grace offered, thus explicitating our Lord's words 'without me you can do nothing', and giving an exposition of St Paul's 'our sufficiency is from God'. He emphasized the gratuity of God's gift of grace and the fact that we cannot know now the whys and wherefores of what he does. The divorce between theology and spirituality which began with the rise of scholasticism in the twelfth century had not taken place, and the ambiguities in Augustine's teaching only became really apparent later. Could grace be irresistible? If so, what became of man's free will? Is one man offered sufficient grace and another not? If so, is God's foreknowledge of the choice equivalent to predestination to Heaven or Hell? Calvin and most of the Protestant reformers and the Jansenists (Catholic heirs of the Donatist rigidity) in the sixteenth and seventeenth centuries leant towards a literal interpretation of predestination, and claimed, not without some justification, support from St Augustine; what they did not realize is that one cannot ask a seventeenth-century question of a fifth-century doctor.

The time for an almost clinical analysis of the spiritual life had not yet come, and there is a breadth and depth in Augustine's teaching that the mystics and doctors of later times never quite reached. He puts before us the fundamentals of the spiritual life: 'God made us to know him, to love him, and to serve him in this world and to be forever happy in the world to come.' Morality is not an external series of laws, to be transgressed at one's peril – a sort of Highway Code – but is summed up in the answer our Lord gave to the scribe who asked which was the greatest commandment. The law of love, written in our hearts, keeps us from sin, but if from weakness we fall we have only to turn back in sorrow, and that love 'which did not spare his only Son' will forgive us and restore us to his household. In his great book *On the Trinity*, in his weighty *City of God*, he shows us the ineffable majesty and power of God, but this Lord and Creator is never alien to us: it is because he has made us for himself that our heart is restless till it rests in him.

It is perhaps in the *Confessions* that we get the key to the man and his teaching. He looks back twelve years after his baptism to what he now sees himself to have been, and traces the path along which God's dynamic love had led him through the vicissitudes of a headstrong adolescence and the anguished search for truth of the brilliant young man he became. Nowhere as in this autobiography do we get a clearer picture of the man, his background and his journey, his home and his friends. In his search for wisdom his staff had been Greek philosophy – especially the Neoplatonism of Plotinus – with its longing for the beautiful, the good and the true, and he describes how he came at last to where they find in God their ultimate expression. Inevitably he sees the sins and weaknesses of the past with the hindsight of maturity, but there is something more fundamental in his estimate. It is often said that Augustine makes too much of a boyhood misdemeanour of robbing an orchard: but this is to misunderstand a whole aspect of his thought. He saw in that wrongdoing, trivial in itself, the very essence of sin; he had said 'evil be thou my good', and in doing so had turned away from God, his first beginning and his last end; he had been faced with a fundamental option.

His famous phrase 'Love, and do what you will' epitomizes his teaching: the love of God and our neighbour is the plumb line and measuring rod of our righteousness in this world as it will be of our eternal happiness; and with every human talent Augustine shows us how to make the journey to where we shall hear our Lord say 'come ye blessed of my Father, receive the kingdom prepared for you'.

He was not, of course, infallible. Loving and beloved as he was, he had no experience of the mutual love of husband and wife, and one has the impression that his sexual experience was 'the expense of spirit in a waste of shame'. His doctrine on sexuality seems to have sprung from that, possibly unconsciously influenced by the dualism of his Manichaean period with the essentially evil material principle in conflict with spiritual good. To Augustine conjugal relations were not merely ordained for the procreation of children, but only allowable, one might almost say excusable, with that intention actually or virtually in mind. So great was his influence through the centuries that the line he traced out became unfortunately the usual Christian outlook, if not formal teaching, until comparatively recent times.

When Eraclius, the successor he had nominated, stood up to preach before the old bishop seated in his chair, he said 'the cricket chirps: the swan is silent', and at the end of Augustine's life it must have seemed that his work would be destroyed. The Vandals were Arians, and would throw out the Catholic bishops and oppress the faithful, and never again would North Africa be the secure civilized country he had been born in, and which had been the temporal background of his teaching. But what he could not know was that down the ages his writings would inspire the learned, and his words find an echo in the hearts of ordinary men and women, the successors of the 'Beloved' whose shepherd he had been.

DAME MAURA SÉE
Stanbrook Abbey
Worcester

The heart at rest

Ask the beauty of the earth, the beauty of the sea, the beauty of the sky. Question the order of the stars, the sun whose brightness lights the day, the moon whose splendour softens the gloom of night. Ask of the living creatures that move in the waves, that roam the earth, that fly in the heavens.

Question all these and they will answer, 'Yes, we are beautiful'. Their very loveliness is their confession of God: for who made these lovely mutable things, but he who is himself unchangeable beauty?

Too late have I loved you, O beauty ever ancient ever new, too late have I loved you.

I sought for you abroad, but you were within me though I was far from you. Then you touched me, and I longed for your peace, and now all my hope is only in your great mercy.

Give what you command and then command what you will.

You have made us for yourself, and our heart is restless till it rests in you. Who will grant me to rest content in you? To whom shall I turn for the gift of your coming into my heart so that I may forget all the wrong I have done, and embrace you alone, my only good?

What sort of prayer?

A man calls on God that he may not be put to confusion. Is it so that the adultery he intends may come off? that someone he hopes to inherit from may die? that a piece of sharp practice may succeed? This is not to call on God, but on one's own evil desires.

To call on God is to invite him into your heart: but will you dare to invite so great a Father when you have no dwelling fit for him? Your heart is full of evil desires, and yet you invite him in.

If you call on God, let it not be to ask for anything. For when you call upon God for aid the call you make is for him to come into yourself. What place is there into which your Lord and God can come, what place fit for the God who made heaven and earth? Is it a small thing that God himself should fill you?

If he comes without silver and gold, do you not want him? Which of the things he has made can satisfy you, if God himself does not?

Come, you blessed of my Father, receive a kingdom

What are we to receive? A kingdom. For doing what? 'I was hungry and you fed me.' What is more ordinary, more of this world, than to feed the hungry, and yet it rates the Kingdom of Heaven!

'Feed the hungry, take the homeless into your house, clothe the naked.' But what if you can't afford bread for the hungry, or have no house nor spare clothes? Give a cup of cold water, put two pence in the alms box. The poor widow gave as much with her two pennies as Zacchaeus did with half his fortune.

What you have is the measure of your gift. Yet many give alms to a beggar to show off, and not because they love their brother.

You stand before God: ask your own heart, look at what you did and why you did it: was it for the empty praise of men? Look at your heart, because you cannot judge what you do not see.

So, beloved, let us search our hearts in God's presence: you can hide from man, but not from God.

Flee to God himself if you want to run away from him; flee by confessing, not by hiding; say to him, 'You are my refuge', and so let the love which alone brings life grow within you.

Works of mercy

Two works of mercy set a man free: forgive and you will be forgiven, and give and you will receive.

When we pray we are all beggars before God: we stand before the great householder bowed down and weeping, hoping to be given something; and that something is God himself.

What does a poor man beg from you? Bread. What do you beg from God? – Christ, who said, 'I am the living bread which came down from heaven'.

Do you really want to be forgiven? Then forgive. Do you hope to receive something? Then give to another. And if you want your prayer to fly up to God, give it two wings, fasting and almsgiving.

But look carefully at what you do: don't think it is enough to fast if it is only penance for sin, and does not benefit someone else. You deprive yourself of something, but to whom do you give what you do without?

Fast in such a way that you rejoice to see that dinner eaten by another; not grumbling and looking gloomy, giving because the beggar wearies you rather than because you are feeding the hungry.

If you are sad when you give alms, you lose both bread and merit, because 'God loves a cheerful giver'.

Be of good cheer

Do not despair of yourselves. You are men, made in the image of God, and he who made you men was himself made man; the blood of the only begotten Son was shed for you. If, thinking of your frailty, you hold yourselves cheap, value yourselves by the price that was paid for you.

I ask you what you believe in, not what you live up to: you will answer that you believe in Christ.

Your faith is your righteousness; because if you believe, you are on your guard, if you are on your guard, you try; and God knows your endeavour and sees your good will, and waits for your striving, and supports your faintness, and crowns your victory.

The Lord knows who are his own, like the farmer who sees the grain among the chaff. Don't be afraid that you will not be recognized, that storms will blow the grain under the chaff. The judge is not some countryman with a pitchfork, but the triune God. He is the God of Abraham, Isaac and Jacob, but he is your God too. You ask him for your reward and the giver is himself the gift. What more can you want?

The grasp of faith

The apostles saw the Lord himself and have told us the words they heard from his lips. We have heard those words too, but have not seen the Lord. Are we then less happy than they who both saw and heard him? How can we have fellowship with them? Is it possible? Yes, because we hold the same faith.

You remember that one of the disciples would not believe unless he touched the wounds: he did, and cried out, 'My Lord and my God'. Touching the man, he acknowledged the Godhead.

And to comfort us who reach by faith him who sits in the heavens, the Lord said, 'Because you saw, you believed: blessed are they who have not seen and yet have believed'.

Beloved, he is speaking to us: let us attain to the bliss he promised by holding fast to what we cannot see, for though we can no longer see him with our eyes, he has not gone away from our hearts, and you believe in him, though you do not see him. You long for his coming again, and yet you know that in his hidden mercy he is still with you, because he said, 'Lo, I am with you always till the end of time'.

The imitation of Christ

Pride is the great sin, the head and cause of all sins, and its beginning lies in turning away from God. Beloved, do not make light of this vice, for the proud man who disdains the yoke of Christ is constrained by the harsher yoke of sin: he may not wish to serve, but he has to, because if he will not be love's servant, he will inevitably be sin's slave.

From pride arises apostasy: the soul goes into darkness, and misusing its free will falls into other sins, wasting its substance with harlots, and he who was created a fellow of the angels becomes a keeper of swine.

Because of this great sin of pride, God humbled himself, taking the nature of a servant, bearing insults and hanging on a cross. To heal us, he became humble; shall we not be ashamed to be proud?

You have heard the Lord say that if you forgive those who have injured you, your Father in heaven will forgive you. But those who speak the world's language say, 'What! you won't revenge yourself, but let him boast of what he did to you? Surely you will let him see that he is not dealing with a weakling?' Did the Lord revenge himself on those who struck him? Dying of his own free will, he uttered no threats: and will you, who do not know when you will die, get in a rage and threaten?

The two commandments

Keep this always before you: that you are to love God and your neighbour. The love of God is the first to be commanded, but the love of your neighbour is the first to be fulfilled.

You cannot yet see God, but you earn the right to see him by loving your neighbour; and looking at the source of that love, you will see God as much as you can now.

Remember that in Christ you have everything. Do you want to love God? You have him in Christ. Do you want to love your neighbour? You have him in Christ, for 'the Word was made flesh'.

You know that the perfection of love is to love your enemy, but at least take great care that you do not hate your brother – if you love only your brother you are not perfect, but if you hate him where are you? What are you? Search your hearts.

Do not bear a grudge because of a harsh word, don't sink down to the level of the earth because of a quarrel over earthly things.

Do not imagine that if you hate your brother you live in Christ and walk in the light. 'The man who says he is in the light and yet hates his brother is still in the dark.'

A Conversion

The very toys of toys and vanities of vanities still held me; they plucked at the garment of my flesh and whispered softly, 'Will you cast us off for ever? and from that moment shall we no longer be with you – for ever?', and I hesitated, for a strong habit said to me, 'Do you think you can live without them?'

But continence said to me, 'Why do you rely on yourself and so waver? Cast yourself upon him, fear not, he will not withdraw himself and let you fall; he will receive you and heal you'.

So I rose and, throwing myself down under a certain fig tree, wept bitterly in contrition of heart. Suddenly I heard from a neighbouring house the voice of a child, singing over and over again, 'Take up and read, take up and read'.

Checking my weeping I got up and went back to where I had been sitting, and had laid down the volume of the apostle, and read the first passage which met my eyes: 'Not in rioting and drunkenness, not in impurity and wantonness, not in strife and envy; but put on the Lord Jesus Christ, and make no provision for the flesh, to fulfil its lusts.'

I needed to read no further, for suddenly, as it were by a light infused into my heart, all darkness vanished away.

Brickbats

Many Christians lead evil lives and insult a man who wishes to live a good life among them: to be sober among drunkards, chaste among fornicators worshipping God sincerely. They will sneer and say, 'You are a great man, you are an Elijah, you are a Peter, and have come down from Heaven'.

So they insult you, and if you get frightened and leave the way of Christ, you fall into the hunter's trap.

How can you hold on? Say to yourself, 'These words are said to me, a servant, a sinner. To my Lord they said, "Thou hast a devil"'.

Begin to live like a Christian, and see if your doing so is not brought up against you by those who are Christians in name but not in life.

Do you wish to follow in the footsteps of your Lord? Then hope in God, and do not blush for that hope even in the sight of men. He lives in your heart: let him then be on your lips.

His sign has been placed on your forehead so that as a Christian you should never blush to be reproached for the name of Christ.

Darkness and light

'God is light, and in him is no darkness', and our salvation lies in fellowship with him. Sin is darkness and our sins keep us from the light which is God. A sort of desperate sadness creeps into our hearts: what shall we do? I live in sin and wickedness, how shall I become light?

Beloved, listen – 'The blood of Jesus Christ his Son will purify us from all sin'. All sin? In baptism our past sins were all wiped out, but living as we do amid the temptations of the world, have we not sinned again? How shall we come to the light?

'If we confess our sins he will forgive us, and cleanse us from all iniquity'; not only our past sins, but the present ones which no one living in this world altogether avoids.

But don't consider lesser sins unimportant: they may not weigh heavy, but tremble when you count them.

Where then is our hope? In acknowledging our sins. Try hard not to sin, but if from weakness you fall, be sorry, realize what you have done, blame yourself: then you can with confidence come before your judge; he is also your advocate and the propitiation for our sins.

Not here, not here

There is only one thing you can be sure of: that you will die; everything else in this life, good or bad, is uncertain except death.

Wherever you turn there is uncertainty; only death is sure, but even the day of your death is uncertain.

We are wanderers with no permanent home on earth; that is in Heaven, and we do not know when we shall hear, 'Come, set out for home'.

Only let us be ready. We shall be, if we long now for our true fatherland.

And yet only with difficulty, because of our weakness, can we unceasingly direct our hearts and works to God. We try to find something in this world to rest in, to pause and lie down.

I do not mean the resting places lovers of evil seek: foul amusements, cheating others, a life of luxury.

No – look at the good man: he seeks his whole refreshment in his family, in a humble life, in the house he has built for himself; these are the satisfactions of the innocent.

But our all embracing love must be for eternal life, and so God allows bitterness to be mixed with these things. Don't be upset when these innocent pleasures have their trials; the man journeying to his own country must not mistake the inn for his home.

Lord, that I may see

We are like people with weak sight who come to a bright light and are beaten back by the glare. They say, 'I did see for a minute, but now I can't'. The physician applies sharp eye salve to foster their hope of seeing.

Brethren, if something like this has happened to you, if somehow you have raised your hearts to look on the Word and, beaten back by its light, you have fallen down to your usual ways, ask him to apply sharp salves.

What are they? The precepts of righteousness: do not lie, do not swear falsely, do not commit adultery, do not steal, do not cheat. You are used to doing these things, and it hurts to give up old habits, but this is what will heal you.

If you give up the healing process, no longer caring to enjoy the light and loving the dark, you will remain in darkness; and by living in darkness now you will be cast into outer darkness where there will be wailing and gnashing of teeth.

Let us love the light, long to understand it and thirst after it so that led by it we may come to it, and there live for ever.

Who can save us?

There are those who rely on their important friends or their own abilities, and others on their wealth – a presumption common to man. But do you really suppose that another man can save you from the wrath to come? The psalmist says, 'his brother shall redeem him', but who is this brother? It is he who after his resurrection said, 'Go and tell my brothers'.

When we call God our Father we are calling Christ our brother, and so need not fear the evil day, since we are not relying on ourselves or our powerful friends but on him who died for us so that we might not die an eternal death, who humbled himself that we might be raised up.

If Christ be not our redeemer who can save us?

For even if a man has led a holy life, it will go hard with him if you put aside your mercy when he stands before you. But you do not search out our sins in anger, and so we believe that one day our home will be with you. This is our hope, but let us know ourselves.

If we reckon up our deserts they are only a list of your gifts; and let us not say we have no debt to pay, in case the devil should prove us wrong, and take us to himself.

Let us answer that our debt has been paid by Christ, that holy victim we receive at your altar, in whom we have triumphed over the enemy.

14

The Body of Christ

Let us live in him since we are his members; let him dwell in us whose temple we are.

The love which is poured into our hearts by the Holy Spirit makes us one body: let us love this unity and fear separation. There is nothing a Christian should be so afraid of as to be separated from the body of Christ: if that happens, he is no longer one of his members nor does he live by his Spirit.

There are many Christians, but only one Christ. Christians themselves, along with their head, form one Christ because he has ascended into Heaven. We are many and he is one, but the many are one in him. There is one man, Christ, consisting of head and body.

Understand what has been God's grace for us! Rejoice and give thanks that we are not only Christians but Christ himself; for if he is the head, we are his members: he and we are the whole man.

The fullness of Christ is head and members – Christ and the Church. He did not wish to separate himself from us, but deigned to attach himself to us, becoming 'God-with-us' that we might be with him.

He was far from us, very far indeed; what can be so far apart as creature and creator, God and man, justice and iniquity, eternal life and mortality? How then did he come near, that he might be in us and we in him? 'The Word was made flesh, and dwelt amongst us.'

The journey

But remember, if you follow the path Christ took, don't promise yourself the good things of this world; he walked by a rough road – follow him.

Reflect on the reward he has promised, and then what you suffer now cannot be compared with what is in store for you. This life is short even if it is passed in labours and trials, and when these are over comes unending happiness.

If you are truly a Christian don't despise the path Christ took: choose to follow him in his sufferings, looking for no other road than his.

It seems a hard way, but it is a safe one: there is another, easy one, but it is infested with terrorists.

When you are our strength we are strong, but when it is our own we are weak.

Let us come home at last to you O Lord, so that we shall not be lost. We are not afraid of there being no home to come back to, though we fell away from it; for our home is your eternity, and it does not fall because we are not there.

There we shall be still and see; seeing we shall love; seeing and loving, we shall praise him. This will come to pass in the end, in that kingdom which will have no end.

A sacrifice

What sacrifice can I offer to God that is worthy of his mercy? Shall I look for a victim from among my herds? No, I will freely offer a sacrifice of praise. Freely: for his sake alone, not for any other reason.

If you praise him for anything else you do not praise him freely. Understand what I mean: suppose you praise God so that he may make you rich. If your riches could be acquired any other way, you would not praise him.

By all means ask him for what will profit you for all eternity, but love and praise him for himself alone. 'Praise his name for he is good' – not for any other reason.

Remember God does not ask of us anything he has not already given us. He does not say, 'Look at your fields and herds and see what you can offer me as a holocaust'.

A holocaust is an offering wholly consumed by fire, and love itself is a blazing fire. When the soul is on fire with the love of God it draws the whole man to its purpose, leaving no room for lesser loves.

If you want to offer him the holocaust of which he has said, 'It is ever before my eyes', be ablaze with divine love, thanking him for giving you whatever is good in you and for forgiving you whatever is evil.

The fool

'The fool says in his heart there is no God.' Few men actually say this, but consider the crowd of evil-doers, people lost to shame, and the Christians living among them who are afraid to reprehend them lest the voice of the virtuous be drowned by the cries of the wicked.

If you say in your heart, 'Oh well, God takes wickedness for granted', it is tantamount to saying, 'There is no God', for wickedness offends him, since if he exists he is righteous.

Scripture (which cannot err) says Christ will come to judge the world – but evil-doers say, 'He will come to forgive us all, it's not true that he will say to us: "Go into everlasting fire prepared for the devil and his angels" '.

Brethren, how could this be? It is a lie. It is saying, 'There is no God'. Take care to hold on to the truth, for he is a righteous God.

You may say, 'I am no thief', 'I am not an adulterer', but if you count such among your friends, if you take pleasure in their life style even if you don't share in it, you are taking part in their deeds.

When you know of evil, and far from blaming it you compound it by saying nothing, so as not to give offence, 'wickedness and deceit are on your lips'.

The alternatives

There are two cities: the earthly city which consists in the love of self even to the contempt of God, and the heavenly city which is the love of God even to the contempt of self.

Consider these two cities, Jerusalem, a vision of peace, and Babylon, called confusion: they are made by two loves, love of God and love of the world. Let each of you ask himself which is his love, and he will know of which city he is a citizen.

There are two births: one of earth and the other of Heaven, one of mortality and the other of eternity, one of human parents, the other of God and the Church.

Who are born of the flesh? Lovers of this world, of this life. For the root of all sin is to turn away from the unchangeable things of God to what is mutable and unsure. Who are born of the Spirit? Lovers of the Kingdom of Heaven, those who long for eternal life.

In this life there are two loves fighting each other in every temptation: love of God and love of the world, and whichever wins draws its lover in its train as by a weight.

The serpent's head

What is the serpent's head? The first suggestion of sin. Some unlawful deed comes into your mind – throw it out, don't consent to it, stamp on the serpent's head.

But he suggests wealth: a little fraud and you'll be a rich man – tread the suggestion underfoot. But you'll make a great deal of money. Brethren, reflect – 'what shall it profit a man to gain the whole world and suffer the loss of his own soul'. Hold on to this and you will bruise the serpent's head.

Only remember, the devil is looking for your heel to strike at. How? If you move away from the path to God by cherishing the evil suggestion he wounds your heel; if you slide right away you will fall, and if you fall he's got you.

There is only one way not to fall, and that is to keep to the strait path to God; anything else is slippery. Christ is your light and your path, the true light which enlightens everyone coming into the world; and he has said, 'I am the Way, by me you journey, to me you come'. If you go away from him you are off the right road and in the dark. It is said of the wicked 'their paths are slippery and dark'.

People say 'Why is the devil so powerful in the world?' Beloved, he can do nothing he is not permitted to do. If he is allowed to tempt you, make him retire in defeat instead of making you his prisoner.

The devil

Before the coming of Christ the devil roamed about: then the Lord came and bound him. Someone may say, 'If he is bound, why does he so often prevail?' It is perfectly true, brethren, he does often prevail; but it is the tepid and careless, and those who do not really fear God, that he overcomes.

He is tied up like a dog on a chain, and can only bite someone who, deathly sure of himself, goes near him. Wouldn't you think a man a fool who let himself be bitten by a chained up dog?

He can only bite those who willingly let him. It is not by force, but by persuasion, that he harms: he asks for our consent, he does not drag it from us.

Fools think that while we need God for eternal life, the powers of this world must be worshipped for its goods. Brethren, God does not share his worship with evil spirits. 'What', you say, 'surely we must take them into account? They might do us harm.'

No, they can do nothing unless he permits it; and if you want to know how futile it is to pay them homage, ask yourselves whether those who pray to Neptune are never shipwrecked.

God is the giver of everything the world can offer and will succour you here and make you happy for ever in Heaven.

Perseverance

Some of the things our Lord Jesus Christ foretold have come to pass, others we still wait for; they will all happen, whether we believe in them or not; and so, dearly beloved, nourish in your hearts the faith that is yours.

In our fathers' times the blood of the righteous was shed, and from that seed the Church grew up.

The devil then, like a lion, raged openly; now he is like a wily serpent. We must defeat him as the martyrs did; suffering was their weapon, watchfulness must be ours.

The Church will always be persecuted, whether by the lion or the serpent, and the enemy is more to be feared when he deceives than when he rages. The Christians were pressed to deny Christ – now they are taught to: violence then, snares now.

What shall we do? With his help let us persevere to the end.

Do not be misled by unbelievers, or, who are more dangerous, bad Christians. The Church is like a net cast into the sea, which gathers up all kinds of fish and is being pulled towards that shore which is the end of this world.

Separate yourselves from the evil fish; not in body but in heart; not by breaking out of the net, but by changing your way of life; so that when the fish are separated on the shore, yours may be not eternal punishment but eternal life.

A ship in danger

There is, as it were, a double aspect: man and sinner. To be a man is God's work, to be a sinner is our doing. Blot out what you have done, so that God may restore what he has done; hate your own work in yourself and love what he has done in you.

Run, my brethren, lest the darkness lay hold of you: wake up while it is daylight, for Christ is the day. He is ready to forgive your sins if you acknowledge them: even if you are free from grave sins, acknowledge those that seem to be small and come to the light.

Bilge water neglected in the hold does the same as a rushing wave: gradually it seeps in and if it is not pumped out sinks the ship. What is this pumping out? To sorrow, to give, to forgive, so that sin may not overwhelm us. But when you see how imperfect you are, don't be afraid – only don't cherish your imperfections and so stick at the point where God found you.

Hold on as much as you can, every day draw nearer to God, and do not hold back from the body of the Lord nor shrink from being friends with Christ. He wants to be a guest in your house; make a place for him. What does that mean? Love him, not yourself. Self-love shuts the door against Christ, to love him opens it; and if you open the door he comes in and you will find yourself with him who loves you.

The new commandment

The Lord said, 'I give you a new commandment: love one another as I have loved you'. By keeping this commandment sin is destroyed; not to love is not only deadly sin but the root of all other sin.

Let no one who does not love his brother think that he is a son of God; and when we look at our sins let us remember that 'love covers a multitude of sins'.

The perfection of love is to be willing to lay down one's life for one's brother, following the Lord's example who died for all men. But does love reach that height all at once? No – when it is born it needs to be nourished, nourished it becomes strong, and strengthened it becomes perfect.

No matter what you have, without love it is worthless; and if you love, nothing is lacking. 'The man who loves his brother has fulfilled the law.'

Don't imagine that you will be forgiven if you don't wholeheartedly forgive.

It is only human to be angry, but the feeble shoot of your anger must not be watered by suspicion and become a bough of hatred. The man who hates his brother is a murderer, and you know that a murderer's heart is empty of eternal life.

The road home

And so, brethren, in this life we are pilgrims; we sigh in faith for our true country which we are unsure about. Why do we not know the country whose citizens we are? Because we have wandered so far away that we have forgotten it. But the Lord Christ, the king of that land, came down to us, and drove forgetfulness from our heart. God took to himself our flesh so that he might be our way back. We go forward through his Manhood so that we may be with him for ever in his Godhead. Do not look for any path to him except himself; for if he had not vouchsafed to be the way we could never have found the path. I do not tell you to look for the way – the way has come to you: arise and walk.

You are not walking on the lake like Peter, but on another sea, for this world is a sea: trials its waves, temptations its storms, and men devouring each other as fishes do. Don't be afraid, step out stoutly lest you sink. Peter said, 'If it is you, bid me come to you on the water'. It was, and he heard his cry and raised him as he was sinking. Gaze in faith at this miracle, and do as Peter did. When the gale blows and the waves rise, and your weakness makes you fear you will be lost, cry out, 'Lord, I am sinking', and he who bade you walk will not let you perish.

The two deaths

As a man you are destined to die. Put it off as long as you like, the thing so long delayed will come at last.

There is however another death, from which the Lord came to deliver us: eternal death, the death of damnation with the devil and his angels. That is the real death; the other is only a change, the leaving of the body.

Do not fear this kind, but be frightened of the other, and labour to live in such a way that after death you may live with God.

Remember that Antichrists are not only to be found among those who have gone away from us, but among many who are still in the Church. The perjurer, the adulterer, the drunkard, the trafficker in drugs, all evil-doers.

They will say, 'But he made us like this'. Our creator cries out from Heaven, 'I made the man, not the thief, the adulterer, the miser; all that moves in the sea, flies in the air, or walks on the earth is my work, and sings my praise'. But does avarice praise the Lord, or drunkenness, or impurity? Anything that does not praise him was not made by him.

If then you love your sins and hug them to yourself you oppose Christ, and whether in the Church or out of it you are an Antichrist: a piece of chaff which the wind will blow away.

Neighbours

My brothers, do not think you must speak the truth to a Christian but can lie to a pagan. You are speaking to your brother, born like you from Adam and Eve: realize that each man is your neighbour even before he is a Christian; you have no idea how God sees him.

The man you mock at for adoring stones may be converted, and may worship God more fervently than you who laughed at him. Some who are not yet in the Church are near to us, and some hidden there are far away. You cannot see into the future, so let every man be your neighbour.

Suppose you saw someone walking in the dark and you knew of an open well into which he might fall and didn't warn him – you would rightly be held an enemy of his soul. And yet, if he fell in, only his body would die. If you see him falling into sin, and you chuckle over it – what then?

It is by love alone that the sons of God are distinguished from the children of the devil. A man can be baptized and so reborn but let him look into his heart and see if he loves his neighbour, and if so he can say truly, 'I am a child of God'.

But if not, though he has received the character of the sacrament, he is no better than a deserter or a vagabond. Only those who love their brethren are children of God.

The slope

A snake does not creep on with open steps; in the same way the slippery motion of falling away takes hold of the negligent man gradually. Beginning with the desire to be godlike, he ends in the likeness of a beast.

The true glory of man is the image and likeness of God, which we can only preserve in our relationship with him who created it; the less therefore one loves oneself the more closely one cleaves to God.

When a man wishes to try out his own strength, he slips down to a purely human level; then, wishing to be subject to none, he falls even lower to those things in which the beasts delight, and so learns the difference between the good he has abandoned and the evil to which he has committed himself.

Only the grace of his maker calling him to repentance and forgiving him enables him to come back.

What can an evil man do when anguish falls upon him? All external resources have failed and he has no peace in his own heart: none of this world's goods can comfort the man who has not God.

The sinner finds no rest outside himself; and, within, his conscience gives him no relief.

A man can fly from an enemy, but who can fly from himself?

Much too risky

When a Christian begins to think of setting out on a more perfect life, he will suffer from the tongues of his opponents. If anyone does not find this so he is not trying to advance.

Listen to what I mean: if he wants to despise the things of this world and the happiness they bring; he will have to put up with contradiction and mockery, and, what is worse, advice from people who would lead him away from salvation. Men with lying tongues will say, 'What, do you propose to do this? No one else does. Do you think you are the only Christian?' And if he points out that others do, and shows them our Lord's words in the Gospel, they will say with guile, 'You'll never carry it through, it's far too much to undertake; oh yes, some people have, but perhaps you won't be able to. If you try to climb up you'll fall'. It sounds like sensible advice, but it's the voice of the serpent with poison under his tongue. Turn to God and say, 'Lord deliver my soul from these lying tongues'. He will answer, 'Can you not do what others have done? Women, rich men brought up in luxury, sick people?'

You will say to him, 'Yes, but I am a sinner; in the past I have sinned greatly'. True: but in the Gospel we read 'he to whom little is forgiven loves little' and so they love him more to whom more has been forgiven. The country you wish to set out for won't be reached without victory against evil: but think how glorious a country it is.

The river of time

 One can love the world, or love God: if we love the world there is no room in our heart for the love of God; we cannot love God and the world, which passes away with its loves.

You ask, 'Why should I not love the world, since God made it?' Brethren, a man loves God too little who loves anything except for God's sake: it is not that created things may not be loved, but to love them for themselves is cupidity, not love.

Choose: either love the things of time, and pass away with them, or do not love them, and live for ever with God.

The river of time sweeps on, but there, like a tree planted by the water, is our Lord Jesus Christ. He became man, willing to plant himself by the river of time.

If you feel yourself drifting down to the rapids, lay hold of the tree; if you are caught up in the love of the world, hold on to Christ. He for your sake entered into time, but he did not cease to be eternal.

The unprofitable servant

I call upon you, O God, my mercy, you who created me, and did not forget me when I forgot you. Let me know you, for you are the God who knows me; you are the power of my soul, come into it and make it fit for yourself. This is my hope.

I beg you to come into my heart, for by inspiring it to long for you, you make it ready to receive you.

Now as I call upon you, do not desert me, for you came to my aid before I called for you. When I was far from you, you persuaded me to listen to your voice, to turn back to you.

I called upon you for help, but all the time it was you who were calling me to yourself. You blotted out all my sins and did not repay me with the punishments I deserved.

I was nothing, you need not have given me being; before I was you were, you had no need of me. My service has not the value of a countryman's who tills his master's land, for if I do not serve you with my labour, your work still bears fruit.

I can only serve you and worship you with the good that comes from you. It is from you alone that I receive it, for but for you I should have no being.

Is it worth it?

Brethren, remember what God has promised us – eternal life. Let no one lead you astray to your death, long for eternal life.

What can the world offer you?

But you answer, 'I am urged to sin by someone powerful, and I am afraid of his threats'. What does he threaten? Prison, tortures, wild beasts, flames? Are those flames eternal?

My brothers, tremble before the Almighty's threats, long for what he promises you and then you will hold cheap anything the world can threaten or promise.

You ask what your reward will be. You say, 'What I have heard from the beginning I keep hold of, I obey. I put up with labours, dangers, temptations, the body which weighs down the soul, all this in order to keep the faith. What will be my reward?'

Listen, beloved, and take courage: if trials seem about to overwhelm you, think of what you are promised, obey him who is Truth itself and whose word cannot fail.

Remember what will be said to those whom he places at his right hand, 'Come, you blessed of my Father, inherit the Kingdom', but to those on his left, 'Depart, you cursed, into everlasting fire'. If you do not as yet long for his promises, at least be afraid of his threats.

The debtor

We must flee to God in our many tribulations, whatever they may be – domestic worries, ill health, dangers to those dear to us. The Christian can have no other refuge but his Saviour, his God. He will have no strength in himself, but in him in whom he has taken refuge.

Yet, beloved, among all human tribulations none is greater than to be conscious of one's sins. If one's conscience is at peace, one can turn into one's heart and there find God.

But if because of the multitude of his sins his heart has no rest and God is not there, where can a man fly in tribulation? If he flies from the country to the town, from the market place to his home, anguish follows him.

Wherever he goes he finds his enemy – wherever he goes he drags himself with him – no troubles are more bitter than those of conscience.

But even there, God comes to our aid by pardoning our sins, and our healing lies only in his forgiveness. If a man owes a great sum of money, he is very much afraid of what will befall him – his only hope lies in being forgiven the debt. How much greater the fear of knowing that we shall perish in paying the debt of our sins.

Beloved, we may be sure of his forgiveness, only let us not incur that debt again.

Don't believe him

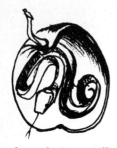

The psalmist says, 'Thou hast shown us thy mercy among the people', but some people say to themselves, 'That could only apply to a few, to hardly anyone – will God be content that a multitude should be lost? If we lead evil lives, revel in this world's pleasures, are slaves of our desires, will God let us perish? Will he only set free the few who keep his commandments, and condemn all the others?' 'Of course not', they say, 'When he comes and sees such a vast multitude on his left hand, he will have pity on them and forgive them.'

Brethren, that was what the serpent said to the first man. God had threatened him with death if he ate the fruit, and the serpent said, 'Of course not, you won't die'. Adam believed him and then found that what God had threatened was true, and what the devil promised was a lie. So don't listen to that sort of talk.

Don't suppose that the good are few in number – there are a great many, but they are hidden among many evil-doers. It cannot be denied that there are so many wicked men that the virtuous may seem concealed like grain in the chaff.

But if you want to find out who are the good, live virtuously yourself and then you will find them.

The jumping-off place

The Lord himself has told us in what the perfection of charity consists: 'Greater love has no man, than to give his life for his friends.' But how can one attain to that level of love?

Well, now we know where its perfection lies, let us see where it begins. St John says if a man is rich, and sees his brother in need and hardens his heart, the love of God is not in him. That is where charity begins. If you can't as yet lay down your life for your brother, at least give him some of your goods – not to show off but from overflowing mercy.

He, your brother, was redeemed as you were by the blood of Christ: he is hungry, in need, perhaps pressed by a creditor, and you have plenty of this world's goods. You say, 'That's no affair of mine. Am I expected to rescue him from distress with my money?'

If that is your attitude, your heart is empty of God's love, you are not a child of God.

You glory in being a Christian – yes, that is what you are called but not what your deeds answer to. If you don't live like a Christian what is the point of being called one?

We shall see him as he is

By the world, brethren, I mean those who love the world, the evil-doers who do not know the righteous as they did not know him who came into the world.

How was this? Because he confronted them with their sins; they revelled in the pleasures of sin and so were unable to see God, for he has said, 'Blessed are the pure of heart, for they shall see God'.

Beloved, we are called to see that which eye has not seen – something far beyond all the beauties of this world, for from that loveliness comes all created beauty. But you may ask, how shall we see him, what shall we be like? Listen: 'We shall be like him, for we shall see him as he is.' Words can tell us no more, the heart alone can understand.

'As he is.' You know of whom 'he is' was said, he who is unchangeable, eternal. Who is he? 'In the beginning was the Word, and the Word was God.' God-made-man will come again to judge the world.

The wicked will look on him whom they pierced. They will not see him as the only begotten Son, the Word equal to the Father, but they will see him as the Word made flesh and hear: 'Depart from me, ye cursed, into everlasting fire.'

Our law

At present our righteousness comes from faith, it is a beginning which the Spirit gives us. It starts when we acknowledge our evil deeds when we no longer try to justify our sins, but it will only reach perfection when death is swallowed up in victory. At the moment we are still in the midst of the battle: we fight and are ourselves wounded. Who will win, we ask ourselves. Brethren, the victor is he who when he fights relies on God who is urging him on, not on his own strength. The devil is skilled in warfare, but if God is with us we shall defeat him. He fights on his own – if we try to do the same he will win. He is an experienced tactician, so call on the Almighty against him. Let the unconquerable one dwell in you, and you will defeat him who usually conquers. Whom does he conquer? Those whose hearts are empty of God.

Love is the fullness of God's law, and the end of his commandments. We have not been given a law which threatens us from outside, but the law of righteousness written in our hearts.

How to love

If the things of this world delight you, turn your love to their creator so that in what pleases you you may not displease him.

If you love people, love them in God because they too are frail and only stand firm when they hold on to him. Love them in him, and draw as many to him as you can.

The world was made by him, and exists in him. Wherever we taste truth, there is God. He is in our very inmost hearts, but we have strayed from him. Cling to him who made you, and peace will be yours.

The good things we love are all from God, but they are good and sweet only when they are used to do his will; they will turn bitter if they are wrongly loved. In this land of death you try to make yourself a happy life. You won't find it there.

Our life himself came down into this world, and took away our death, calling us to return to him in Heaven. He went from our sight, so that we should find him in our hearts.

Your life has come down from Heaven, will you not now at last rise with him and live? But how can you rise if you sit in high places and your clamour reaches to Heaven? Come down from your heights and this time climb to God.

Here today and gone tomorrow

Wherever the soul of man turns, unless it turns to you it clasps sorrow to its heart. Even if it clings to what is lovely, if this loveliness is outside God, it has clung to sorrow, for these beautiful things would not exist without you. Like the sun, they rise and set: they have their beginning and then they grow old and die.

Let me praise you for these things, my God who made them all, but do not let the love of them be like glue to fix them to my soul.

In these things there is nowhere to rest, because they do not last, they pass away beyond the reach of our senses. Indeed we cannot lay firm hold on them even when they are with us.

In this world one thing passes away, and another takes its place. But does the Word of God pass away? Make your dwelling in him. Entrust to him whatever you have, for all you possess is from him. In him is the peace that cannot be disturbed, and he will not withhold himself from your love if you do not withhold your love from him.

My God, my all

Why do you mean so much to me? Why do I mean so much to you that you command me to love you? And if I fail to love you, you threaten me with great sorrow, as if not to love you were not sorrow enough.

Have pity on me and help me, O Lord my God, speak so that I may hear your words. Whisper in my heart, 'I am here to save you'. My heart has ears ready to listen to you, Lord, open them wide and I shall hear your voice and make haste to clasp you to myself.

My soul is like a house, small for you to enter, but I beg you to enlarge it. It is in ruins; I ask you to rebuild it.

In it is much that will displease you: this I know and I do not conceal it from you. But who is to empty it of these things? To you only I can say, 'I trust, and trusting I find words to utter'. Lord, you know that this is so, for I have acknowledged my sin.

I do not dispute your judgement for you are truth itself, and I have no wish to delude myself lest I betray my own malice. 'For if you, Lord, will mark iniquities who may abide it?'

The heart's delight

First return to yourself from what is outside you, and then give yourself back to him who made you; for he is the sum of all our happiness and our perfect good. To worship him is to love him, to long to see him, and to hope and believe that you will see him. This is to long for happiness – to reach him is happiness itself.

Ask yourself how much your love has increased: the answer your heart gives is the measure of your advancement. We now see him confusedly, as our love increases – but then we shall see him clearly.

Beloved, this love does not come to us of our own free choice, but by the Holy Spirit who has been given to us; for how could we have cleaved to God if he had not spoken to our hearts?

At the last we shall all receive the reward of salvation, like the labourers in the vineyard who came at different times, yet all were given the same wage. With the prophets, apostles and martyrs we shall contemplate the glory of God, and looking in his face sing his praises for ever. There will be no more sin, no more falsehood, and in love we shall cleave to him for whom we now sigh. We shall live for ever in that city whose light is God, finding in him that happiness we now labour for.

Calm yourself and reflect

You have heard, 'Be subject to God, and pray to him'. How do you know whether you are? If you obey his commandments. You will say that you have not been rewarded for obeying him. Work in the vineyard, and at the end of the day ask for your wages: he who sent you there will keep his word.

'All very well', you say, 'I obey God and I pray, but what is your answer to this: I have a neighbour who is an evil-doer yet lives in great prosperity. I know him to be dishonest, immoral, and grasping; he is so proud and conceited that he does not even deign to acknowledge my existence. How long am I expected to put up with that situation?'

Here is the remedy for your sickness: 'Do not envy the man who prospers in his way.' Oh yes, he prospers, but in his own way, you labour but in God's path. He journeys gaily, but where will he arrive?

If Christ had promised you this world's goods, by all means be angry at an unbeliever doing well for himself. What did he promise you? Eternal happiness when the dead rise again, and in this life his own lot. I repeat, the road he took; and do you, a servant, a disciple, despise what your master underwent? You have heard that a servant is not greater than his lord. For you he suffered what he, the righteous one, did not deserve. What do you, a sinner, deserve?

In him we live and move and have our being

You were walking in your own ways, a vagabond; straying in the rough places, wooded places, tearing your limbs. You were looking for a home, some rest for your spirit, somewhere where you could say, 'I am all right here', and safely say it, free from anxiety and trials – in other words, be altogether free – but you did not find it.

What then? Did someone come and show you how to get there? The way itself came to you and you were set on it through no merit of your own. You had clearly lost the path. Tell me then, has he who showed you the path deserted you, must you now find your own way home?

Beloved, the end of all our paths is Christ: in him we are made perfect, for our perfection is to come home to him. Don't seek for anything else. He is your end, to him you are journeying, and when you have arrived there you will not seek further, for you can desire nothing better than to come home to him.

He has led us on, he himself being our way, and he brings us to himself as to our home. We come through Christ to Christ, through the Word made flesh to the Word which in the beginning was God with God, for he says to us: I am the way and to me you come.

Believe and then you will know

We believe, not because we know but so that we may come to know. For what we shall know no eye has seen, no ear heard, nor has man's heart imagined. Faith is to believe what we do not yet see: truth to see what we have believed. To follow after God is to long for happiness, to reach him is that happiness itself.

If we have reached the pathway of faith let us keep to it unswervingly, so that our hearts may become able to know those things which at present we do not understand.

Bring the light of reason to bear on what you now believe firmly by faith.

Could God hate in us that by which he has distinguished us from the beasts? Of course not: we could not in any case believe, if we had not reasonable souls.

There are some things belonging to our salvation which we as yet cannot understand, though one day we shall. In these matters faith should go ahead of reason, purifying the heart and making it able to receive the great light of reason.

The prophet said, unless you believe you shall not understand; thus we may see that it is reasonable for faith to go before. If we are persuaded of this, it is by the small amount of reason which goes before faith.

The Pharisee

Shall a Christian go and live apart from the world, so that he may not be tried by false brethren? Shall he who has progressed in a righteous life separate himself from the rest so that he need not suffer from anyone? Perhaps people suffered from him before he was converted. Has no one anything to put up with from you? It would surprise me – but if it is so, then you are stronger and thus able to endure other people's failings.

Do you propose to shut out bad men from good men's company? If that is what you say, see if you can shut out all evil thoughts from your own heart. Every day we fight with our own heart.

You say you will go apart with a few good men and admit no wicked brother to your society. How do you recognize the man you wish to exclude? Do all come to you with their hearts bare? Those who wish to come do not know themselves, they cannot be proved unless they are tried.

Nowhere in this life are we secure, except in God's promise – only when we have attained to it, when the gates of Jerusalem are shut behind us, shall we be perfectly safe.

Beloved, mark the apostle's words: 'Support one another in charity.' You forsake the world of men and separate yourself from it. Whom will you profit? Would you have got so far if no one had profited you?

Treasure hunting

Let the Lord your God be your hope – seek for nothing else from him, but let him himself be your hope. There are people who hope from him riches or perishable and transitory honours, in short they hope to get from God things which are not God himself. Seek for him alone, and despising everything else, make your way to him. Forget other things, remember him; leave other things behind, stretch out to him. Let him be your hope, who is guiding you to your destination.

Where in the end does coveting this world's goods lead you? You want a farm, then an estate, then you shut your neighbours out and covet their possessions. You extend your desires till you reach the shore. Having made the earth your own, perhaps you want heaven, too?

Leave all your desires. He who made heaven and earth is more beautiful than all; he who made all things is better than all; he will be to you everything you love. Learn to love the creator in the creature, in the work him who made it. Don't let what was made take such a hold of you that you lose him by whom you yourself were made.

What have I on earth but thee?

No Christian can say he has no tribulations – why? Because as long as we are in the body, we are only journeying to God. However well off we may be we are not yet in that homeland to which we are hastening. A man cannot love the journey and his own country too. If he loves his country, the journey will seem wearisome and full of tribulations. Here we labour and sorrow: there endless rest and unwearied love.

But, you will say, I have everything I want. Have you? Are you sure that everything won't disappear? But I'm richer than I was, I've made a lot of money: possibly you are more afraid than you were, you might have felt more secure when you were poorer. But suppose you have everything, are rich in this world's goods and feel sure of them too, and moreover God says to you: 'All this will go on for ever, you shall possess these things for ever – but you will never see my face.'

Brethren, ask the spirit, not the flesh. Let faith, hope and charity which are beginning to grow in your hearts give your reply. Think: would all those possessions make us happy if we were never to see his face? God forbid that anyone rest his joy in them and seek for nothing more. Such a man has not begun to love God, to live as a pilgrim. Nothing that we have except God can really be sweet to us. He is the giver of all things; without him himself what are they to us?

With one voice

We read: 'Praise the Lord with me; let us exalt his name together.' To whom is the psalmist speaking? To every member of Christ's body. And what kind of praise does he mean? That which is not jealous of another's love.

The love of the flesh is pestilential. Let a man cast his eyes on a woman's beauty and he desires it for himself alone, and rages at the thought of sharing the sight with someone else. Not so is the love of the wisdom of God. We shall look on him face to face, we shall all see him, and there will be no envying of one another.

He will show himself to all and they shall all be changed but he will not change. He is wisdom, he is God, by whom all things were made. He has his lovers, but note what the lover says: 'Magnify the Lord with me.' Not alone will I magnify him, love him, embrace him. There is room for all men.

In this world men love chariot racing, hunting and so on and want everyone to admire their favourites too. They say, 'Share my love for this dancer, that actress, this obscenity' – that is what the mob clamours.

Does the Christian in the Church cry out that everyone should love the truth of God with him?

Be fervent, brethren; if you love God draw all who are near to you, all your household, to that love.

Freely, freely you have received

To hope that the eternal God will give you this world's goods or the devil everlasting life is equally monstrous. Keep your eye on the ball, keep to the right road.

If your legs are strong so much the better – run – the faster you move, the sooner you will get home. But perhaps you limp a bit? All right, only don't leave the way, you will get there even if a little late. Don't stick on the way or turn back, don't wander off.

What are we to make of this? Are only those who have not sinned blessed? No, those are blessed whose sins are forgiven. That grace is given to us freely: we have no good works to show and yet he forgives us our sins.

If you look at your deeds you see wickedness, and if God rewards them you would be damned, for 'the wages of sin is death'. But see, God does not exact the payment for sin, but gives you freely grace which is not owed to you.

Punishment is your due, forgiveness is what you receive, and with this forgiveness your faith begins, and with his love, you will begin to do right. Only don't glory in yourself, or be puffed up. Remember what you were when he found you. Reflect that you are a sinner, and then realize that through faith by love you have begun to do well, and this not of your own strength but by the grace of God.

Straighten the crooked path

Look at the difference between an upright and a crooked heart. The righteous man realizes that when afflictions or sorrow or humiliations fall on him it is by God's holy will, and so accepts it. The man with a twisted and perverted heart puts up with it angrily. He agrees that he is a sinner, but says there are many worse than he who are happy.

In fact there are three arguments that his crooked heart puts forward: either there is no God – the fool says that – or God is unjust, or God does not rule the lives of men, and disinterests himself in what happens to them. The upright heart accepts whatever happens to him, saying 'The Lord has given, the Lord has taken away; as it pleased him so he has done: blessed be the name of the Lord'.

Your tribulations come from God – a punishment for the sinner, a chastisement for the son. If you wish to be a son, don't expect to escape pains, for 'He chastises every son he receives'. Every son? Without exception?

Listen. The only begotten Son was without sin, and yet he suffered. He took to himself our infirmity, the head bearing the members of the body in his person. As man he went to his Passion sorrowful that you might rejoice, in anguish that you might be consoled. He said, 'My soul is sorrowful even unto death, but not what I will but what you will, Father'.

The life we lead

There are three kinds of life: that of repose, that of action, and the one which combines the two. A man may attain to everlasting happiness by leading any of them, as long as he keeps to the faith.

But we must ask the man who seeks the truth in repose what he does for love of his neighbour. He must not give himself up to idle leisure; let him search for the truth, progress in his search, hold fast to what he has learnt and be generous in sharing it with others. He who leads an active life must not long for honours and power – he must love the work itself if it is well and profitably done, that is, if it leads to the salvation of those under him.

Let no one be so attached to his own repose that he has no thought for his neighbour, nor on the other hand be so busy that he neglects the contemplation of God. If we are believers, we are walking in the path of faith, and if we keep to it, some of us will arrive at a certain comprehension of the unchanging truth, and at the end will contemplate it 'face to face' as the apostle says.

On the other hand, there are those who, while understanding what is meant by things invisible and immutable, refuse to keep to the way that alone leads to everlasting happiness, the way of Christ crucified. Some rays of heavenly light have reached their souls, but only as it were from a great distance, and they will not reach Christ's hidden mansion of rest.

Lift up your hearts

It is foolish to deceive oneself: look into your hearts and acknowledge how often useless thoughts get in the way of your prayer. You want to praise God but you cannot find anything that will restrain your wandering thoughts, so that in all your prayers there is scarcely one that is really prayer.

Only remember that God is gentle and mild and bears with our wandering and waits for us to pray in such a way that he may perfect it. When he gives us that prayer he accepts it and does not remember how badly we have prayed before. If you were before a judge and in the middle of your speech you started gossiping with a friend, what would happen? Yet God puts up with prayers that are interrupted by other thoughts.

When you read, he speaks to you; when you pray, you speak to him.

If this is so, brethren, must we despair, thinking that punishment awaits anyone whose mind wanders at his prayer? No; let us say: 'Rejoice the soul of thy servant, for to thee O Lord I lift up my soul.' How shall I lift it up? As much as I can with the strength you give me; as much as I am able to keep hold of my wandering thoughts. Because you are mild and gentle you do not cast me off; strengthen me and I shall stand firm, and until then bear with me.

Work while it is day

We read in the psalm: 'My sorrow is always before me.' What sorrow? Brethren, let me speak plainly: we sorrow over our misfortunes, but do we consider why they have happened? A man who suffers loss is more likely to say, 'I did not deserve it', than to remember what he did deserve. To mourn the loss of money more than that of righteousness. If you have sinned mourn over the treasury of your heart. Your purse is empty – perhaps your soul is even emptier. God forbid that we should be sorrowful over our pains. Let us regret the wound, not the medicine that heals it, for misfortune is the cure for sin.

Listen, brethren: we are Christians. If one of your children dies, you mourn, but if he sins you do not, and yet in your house he is not only dead, but putrifying. Sin is what we must weep for; we must bear with anything else. The psalm goes on: 'For I acknowledge my wickedness.' Yes, but don't feel secure when you have acknowledged your sins: are you confessing them and going on committing them? A man can weep copiously and do nothing about it.

You want to heal the wound? Then take steps to do so. Redeem your sins by giving alms. The beggar rejoices in your gift, and you in what God has granted you. In your eyes he is a beggar; what are you before God? If you look at him with scorn, how does God see you? That is why I tell you to give him what he needs, so that God may fill your empty heart.

Temptation

Many people when they are first converted are fervent in prayer, but afterwards pray languidly, coldly, and then without paying attention; this because they feel secure. The enemy keeps watch and you are asleep.

Just think for a moment, brethren, how easily you say of a certain man, 'He is an evil-doer, a scoundrel'. Look into your own heart in case you see wickedness there. Are you not prepared to do yourself what you condemn in another?

Return to your heart, there you will be alone with him who sees all things. Hate sin, so that you may please God. Don't cherish it, don't think it over, rather despise it and turn away from it.

Temptation will suggest that sin can make you happy, it will threaten sorrow to tempt you to evil; but all this is emptiness, and will pass away. Wicked suggestions can come by thoughts or by evil conversations, and right living is easily corrupted. Wherever they came from, throw them out of your heart, don't pay attention to them, don't cherish them.

But don't add up your merits: we don't come to Christ from righteousness, we have all sinned, and it is by his inspiration that we accomplish the good he has given us. We must remember what he commanded in his Gospel, 'Pray without ceasing', and if you do not give up prayer you may be sure he will not forget his mercy.

Our first beginning and our last end

He is the truth, the absolute good, and the soul's goodness comes from that same source which has made it; the soul's perfecting in goodness comes from the conforming of its will to its nature, when it turns in love towards that good to which it owes its very existence – an existence which cannot be lost even if the will turns away from its creator.

This good is not far from any of us, for 'in him we live and move and have our being'. But we must cleave in love to it so that we may enjoy the presence of him from whom we have our being.

The apostle says we walk by faith as yet, and not by sight. But unless we already love him, we shall never see him. How can we love what we do not know? To know God is to perceive him with the assured grasp of the mind, and to see and apprehend him is given to the pure in heart. Our hearts however cannot be made pure to see him unless we love him in faith.

Faith, hope and charity are the virtues for whose building the whole scaffolding of Scripture is set up. The soul which believes what it does not yet see, hopes in and loves that which it believes – that is why we can love God if we believe, even before we know him.

The love of God

We need not fly to the height of heaven, nor go down to the depths of the earth, to find him who is with us, if only we love him and want to be with him.

No one need say 'But what am I to love?' Love your brother, and you will be loving love itself, you will know the love by which you live better than the brother whom you love. God can be better known than the brother: better because more present, more inward, and more sure.

Take to your heart the love that is God, through love embrace him. He is that very love that draws together all God's servants, angels and men, uniting them with each other in obedience to himself.

He who is filled with love is filled with God himself.

St John says: 'He who does not love his brother whom he sees, cannot love God whom he does not see.' Why is that? If he does not love his brother he walks in darkness and cannot see the light; he only sees his brother with an outward human vision which cannot see God who is himself the love he lacks. It is with the same love that God and our neighbour are loved, for God is love.

Beatitude

The end of all our action is contemplation as it will be the everlasting perfection of everyone, for God said to his servant Moses, 'I am he who is', and it is him that we shall contemplate in eternal life. For the Lord said, 'This is eternal life: to know Thee the one true God, and Jesus Christ whom thou hast sent'.

This will come to pass when the Lord comes and the darkness and corruption of our mortality vanishes. That will be our tomorrow, when we shall not look for anything else except that joy which we now hope for. We shall not seek greater happiness, for there will be none.

We shall see the Father and that will suffice us. Philip realized this when he asked it of the Lord, but he did not understand that he could have said, 'Lord, show us thyself and it is enough', and so the Lord said, 'He who sees me, sees the Father', and since he wanted him to believe what he did not yet see, he went on: 'Do you not believe that I am in the Father and the Father in me?'

Contemplation is the reward of that faith which purifies our hearts (and it is the pure of heart who will see God). So it does not matter whether we say, 'Show us the Father', or 'Show us the Son': we cannot be shown one without the other, since with the Holy Spirit they are one. Beloved, realize that the joy of all joys will be to delight in the Trinity in whose image we have been created.

Martha and Mary

The Lord said, 'I will see you again, and your hearts will rejoice, and no one shall take your joy away'. Mary prefigured that joy when she sat at the Lord's feet listening to what he said.

She was silent, doing no work, she cleaved to the truth as far as can be in this life, yet it is only a foreshadowing of the joy that will last for ever.

Her sister Martha was occupied with work that has to be done, but which, however good and useful, will pass away when we come to eternal rest. So the Lord said, 'Mary has chosen the best part which shall not be taken from her'. He did not say that Martha's part was bad, only that the one which would not be taken away was the better.

For example, the work of looking after the needy will pass away, when there is no more poverty. But it is the transitory good works that will gain us eternal rest. In contemplating God each of us will find all that we desire, for he will be all in all when we see and possess him; that is why his Holy Spirit in our hearts makes us pray: 'One thing have I asked, this I have longed for: to dwell for ever in the Lord's house and contemplate his love.'

My Lord and my God

Is there anything more valuable than your soul? Nothing indeed, except God himself; apart from him you can find nothing better than your own soul because when you are perfect you will be like the angels, and above them is only their creator. Lift up your heart to him and don't settle for something lower, saying 'Oh, that is beyond me'.

You probably won't get that money you want. It does not at all follow that because you want it you will get it. But if you long for God, you can possess him. Even before you wanted him he drew near you, when you turned away he beckoned you, and when at last you turned to him in fear and confessed your sins in terror, he tenderly consoled you.

Every beautiful thing you see, every fair thing you love was made by God. Looking on all those things, long for him more than for them all. Love him, and purify your heart by faith so that you may come to see him who gave you your being, and all you have.

Remember that he who gave the happiness of this world gave it for our comfort. He gives to all men the sun and the rain, the harvest and the springs of water, and he will give you the gift of himself.

Augustine's prayer

Guiding my mind by the rule of faith, I have sought you with all my heart, with all the power you have given me. I have longed to understand that which I believe.

O Lord my God, my only hope, listen to me. Don't let my weariness lessen my will to seek you, to seek your face for ever.

You made me to find you; give me strength to seek you. My strength and my weakness are in your hands: preserve my strength and help my weakness. Where you have opened the door, let me enter in; where it is shut, open to my knocking.

Let me ever increase in remembering you, understanding you, loving you, until you restore me to your perfect pattern.

Suggestions for further reading

BIOGRAPHY

Augustine of Hippo, Peter Brown (1967). Brilliant, but ignores St Augustine's spirituality.

'Augustine of Hippo', G. Bonner in *Dictionary of Christian Spirituality* (1983)

Augustine the Bishop, F. van der Meer (1961). Keeps to the title, but indispensable reading.

GENERAL

A guide to the thought of St Augustine, E. Portalié (1960)

Amor Dei. A study of the religion of St Augustine, J. Burnaby (1938)

Augustine: Life and Controversies, G. Bonner (1986).

An Augustine Synthesis, E. Przywara (1936)

Introduction to the Spirituality of St Augustine, T. van Bavel (1980)

Pagan and Christian in an Age of Anxiety, E. R. Dodds (1965)

The Rule of St Augustine, tr. Raymond Canning (1984)

St Augustine, K. Adam (1932)

St Augustine, Henry Chadwick (1986)

St Augustine. Pastoral theologian, T. Rowe (1974)

St Augustine on Prayer, H. Pope (1935)

TRANSLATIONS

Comparatively little of Augustine's work has appeared in English, but here are some of the main translations.

Ancient Christian Writers (1946)

Earlier Writings (1953)

Later Writings (1956). Contains 'The Spirit and the Letter' and 'Commentary on the 1st Epistle of St John'.

Letters (1951)

Library of Christian Classics (1951)

Selected Easter Sermons (1954)

Sermons for Christmas and Epiphany (1951–3)

The City of God (many editions)

The Confessions (many editions)

The Fathers of the Church (1947)

The Sermon on the Mount (1946)

The following will probably only be found in a university or specialized library.

Homilies on the Gospel and Epistle of St John (1848)

Library of Post Nicene Fathers (1838–58)

On Christian Doctrine (1873)

Seventeen Short Treatises (1847)

Soliloquies (1912)

Works of St Augustine (1857)

Sources

Source references are to Migne's *Patrologia Latina* from which the translations have been made. The figures in bold type refer to the pages of Readings in this book. They are followed by the Sources.

1 *Sermon 241.* 2.2. 3.3
Confessions. X. 27. 29
ibid. I. 1

2 *Psalm 30.* III. 4
Sermon on New Testament. 105. 3.4

3 *Psalm 49.* 13

4 *Sermon 83 on St Matthew's Gospel* passim
Psalm 43 passim

5 *Psalm 32.* 4
Psalm 49. 15

6 *Commentary on St Matthew's Gospel.* VII. 1

7 *Psalm 37.* 3 and passim
Commentary on St John's Gospel. VII. 7

8 *Commentary on St John's Gospel.* XXVII. 8
Sermon 241. 8
Commentary on 1st Epistle of St John. V. 2.3

9 *Confessions.* VIII. 11.12

10 *Psalm 90.* 4
Psalm 30. II. 7

11 *Commentary on 1st Epistle of St John.* I. 5.6

12 *Psalm 38.* 19.21
Psalm 40. 5

13 *Commentary on St John's Gospel.* XVIII. 34

14 *ibid.* CXXIV passim
Sermon 372
Sermon 141

15 *Sermon 127*
Psalm 30. 4
Commentary on St John's Gospel. XXI. 8

16 *Psalm 36.* II. 16
Confessions. IV. 16
Sermon 256
City of God. XXII. 30

17 *Psalm 53.* 10
Psalm 49. 15

18 *Psalm 52.* 2
Psalm 49. 25.26

19 *City of God.* XIV. 28
Commentary on St John's Gospel. XI. 6
On Free Choice. I. 16
Psalm 64. 2

20 *Psalm 103.* IV. 6.7

21 *Sermon 37*
Psalm 26. 19

22 *Psalm 39.* 1
Commentary on St John's Gospel. XXIII. 10

23 *ibid.* XII. 13.14
Psalm 136. 21
Psalm 131. 5.6